Who Was Kit Carson?

Emma Ericson

INFOMAX
COMMON CORE
READERS

Rosen Classroom™

New York

Published in 2014 by The Rosen Publishing Group, Inc.
29 East 21st Street, New York, NY 10010

Book Design: Jon D'Rozario

Photo Credits: Cover (Carson) Trascendental Graphics/Archive/Getty Images; cover, pp. 5, 7, 11, 15, 17, 19 (paper)
Tischenko Irina/Shutterstock.com; pp. 5, 22 (background) donatas1205/Shutterstock.com; p. 5 (Carson) Underwood
Archives/Archive Photos/Getty Images; p. 7 James Laurie/Shutterstock.com; p. 9 Galyna Andrushko/Shutterstock.com;
p. 11 Time Life Pictures/Time Life Pictures/Getty Images; p.13 trekandshoot/Shutterstock.com; pp.15, 19 Stock Montage/
Archive Photos/Getty Images; p. 17 Kean Collection/Archive Photos/Getty Images; p. 21 Mona Makela/Shutterstock.com.

ISBN: 978-1-4777-2292-3
6-pack ISBN: 978-1-4777-2293-0

Manufactured in the United States of America

CPSIA Compliance Information: Batch #CS13RC: For further information contact Rosen Publishing, New York, New York at 1-800-237-9932.

Contents

A Frontier Hero

In the 1800s, Americans wanted to learn about the lands west of the Mississippi River. They loved to read and hear stories about the people who lived and traveled in the wild places they called the frontier. One of these men was Kit Carson. He was a famous western guide and **soldier**. Many Americans called him a hero!

Kit Carson helped people travel through the frontier. He also fought in wars that helped the United States become the large country it is today.

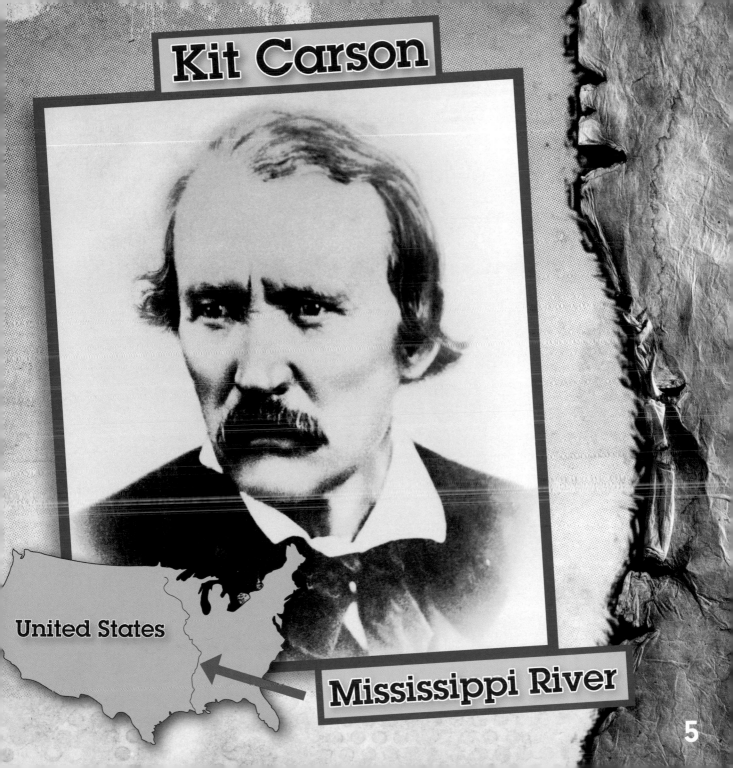

Kit Carson

United States

Mississippi River

Family Life

Kit Carson's real name was Christopher Carson. He was born on December 24, 1809, in Kentucky. Soon after he was born, his family moved to Missouri. Kit came from a big family. He had nine brothers and sisters! After his father died in 1818, Kit had to work on his family's land to help his mother.

Because Kit had to work on his family's land, he couldn't go to school.

Looking for Adventure

When Kit was 14, he left home and became an apprentice to a man who made **saddles** for horses. What's an apprentice? It's a person who works for someone in order to learn a skill. Kit didn't like being an apprentice. He wanted to have **adventures**! In 1826, he ran away to Santa Fe, New Mexico.

What was the West like back then? It was a wild place full of people looking for adventure, just like Kit!

Mountain Man

In New Mexico, Kit learned how to trap animals in order to get their fur. People then sold those furs to make clothing. While he worked as a trapper, Kit traveled all over the West. He made his home in the city of Taos, New Mexico, but he often went as far as California. He even went to the Rocky Mountains!

Life on the frontier was hard, but Kit loved it!

Kit became famous as a "mountain man," which is what Americans called people who lived and worked in wild lands of the West. He couldn't read or write, but he spoke Spanish, French, and several Native American languages. Kit often lived among Native Americans. His first and second wives were members of Native American tribes.

Mountain men like Kit led lives filled with adventures in the West.

Who Was John C. Frémont?

In 1842, Kit met the explorer John C. Frémont. What's an explorer? It's someone who travels through new places. John traveled throughout the frontier and wrote about what he saw. John made Kit his guide for his travels through the West. Kit took John and his group to the South Pass in the Rocky Mountains.

John's writings about his travels were read by many Americans.

John C. Frémont

John and Kit traveled to many places in the West together. Where else did they go? In 1843, they went to Utah. Kit also traveled through California and Oregon with John in 1845. John's reports about his trips through the frontier told how brave Kit was. Kit became a hero. People even wrote books about him!

Americans felt like they knew Kit after they read about him in John's reports.

A Brave Fighter

What other things was Kit known for? He was also a soldier. In 1846, a war broke out between the United States and Mexico. Kit fought bravely in that war to help the United States get more land in the West. Kit also fought in the American Civil War. This was a war between two parts of the United States.

Kit was a brave soldier and a good leader.

19

A Life of Adventure

After the Civil War, Kit moved to Colorado. He died there in 1868. He's remembered as a hero of the frontier who lives on in the stories written and told about his life. Kit dreamed of adventure when he was young, and he had lots of adventures throughout his life!

The Carson National Forest was named after Kit Carson. Where can you find this forest? It's in New Mexico.

What Did He Do?

worker on his family farm

frontier guide

soldier

Who was Kit Carson?

mountain man

fur trapper

apprentice

Glossary

adventure (uhd-VEHN-chur) An exciting trip or event.

saddle (SA-duhl) A seat that a person sits on when they ride a horse.

soldier (SOHL-juhr) A person who fights in a war.

Index